SUSAN GREEN

PICTURES BY GREGORY ROGERS

IT'S TRUE!

fashion can be fatal

ALLEN&UNWIN

For Lachlan and Howard

First published in 2004

Allen & Unwin
83 Alexander Street
Crows Nest NSW 2065
Australia
Phone: (61 2) 8425 0100
Fax: (61 2) 9906 2218
Email: info@allenandunwin.com
Web: www.allenandunwin.com

National Library of Australia
Cataloguing-in-Publication entry:

Green, Susan.
It's true! : fashion can be fatal.
Includes index.
For children aged 8–12 years.
ISBN 1 74114 302 0.
1. Fashion – Juvenile literature. I. Rogers, Gregory, 1957– . II. Title.
391

Series, cover and text design by Ruth Grüner
Cover photograph: Clair Hume
Set in 12.5pt Minion by Ruth Grüner
Printed by McPherson's Printing Group

1 3 5 7 9 10 8 6 4 2

**Teaching notes for the It's True! series are available
on the website: www.itstrue.com.au**

CONTENTS

WHY FASHION?

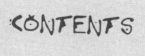

WHY FASHION?

I love watching people and making up stories. Fashion is a great starting point for me, because clothes can tell you so much about people. How about that man in the slick suit . . . is he a businessman, a politician or on his way to a wedding? And the girl dressed all in black. Is she off to a funeral? Who died? I wonder if I'm ever right.

I also love the way fashion can help us understand the past. What they wore shows how people lived and worked, and what they believed and valued. Some men and women virtually lived for fashion. They spent all their money, looked silly, felt embarrassed, or endured pain. I call these people fashion victims and I've put a few of their stories through the book.

Some of them are real, and some of them are made up. The made-up ones are based on history, though. All the fashions – even the unbelievable ones – were actually worn. It's true!

Susan Green

1

CHANGING CLOTHES

HOW FASHION GOT STARTED

For centuries, people didn't change their clothes. No, I don't mean there were very old people getting around in very smelly gear. I mean that the styles didn't change much, and when they did, they changed very slowly.

Poor people wore plain clothes and rich people wore fancy clothes. It was the same all over the world. But in Europe and England at the end of the thirteenth century, people started changing their clothes in a big way. Why?

FASHION EXPLOSION

In the thirteenth century – the 1200s – European cities were booming. People were travelling more, for adventure, war or trade. They brought back new styles and materials from countries as far away as Russia, China and the Middle East. The royal courts were buzzing with artists, poets, writers, musicians, adventurers, diplomats and travellers. More people had money to spend on themselves. Europe's fashion explosion had begun.

Now is a good time to point out that while other places have their share of weird and wonderful fashions, only in Europe did fashions come and go every few years. The basic shape of clothes in countries like Japan, India and China stayed the same for centuries.

KING OF THE CASTLE

At first, fashion was only for wealthy people. Clothes were expensive because everything was done by hand. There were no machines for spinning thread, weaving textiles or sewing. Poor people didn't have the money to spend on luxury materials or impractical styles. But life was very different at court.

'Court' means both the place and the people. The king, queen or ruler lived in a palace with hundreds of other people – family, friends, courtiers, officials and servants. As well as the serious business of government, there were lots of parties, feasts, dances and visitors.

As rulers of the court, kings and queens were expected to dazzle with fancy clothes, jewels and extravagant styles: it was a way of showing that they were powerful and rich. The royals' clothes and hair were often copied by the rest of the court.

Here are some royal fashion stories.

ICECREAM AND UNDERPANTS

All sorts of fashions were introduced to France when Catherine de' Medici (1519–89) left her home in Florence, Italy to marry Henry II of France: Italian cooking, icecream, the fan, the side-saddle and drawers (long underpants). Most women didn't wear any undies at all until the nineteenth century. Catherine wore them while riding to hide her legs and bottom in case she fell. Drawers never really caught on, though. Some people thought wearing drawers was rude, shocking or even wicked.

LIKE A DUCK'S BEAK

Shoes with square tips, like a duck's beak, were launched by Charles VIII of France (1470–98) to hide the fact that he had one very unusual foot. It had six toes.

DRESSY BESSIE

Queen Elizabeth I of England (1533–1603) was a real fashion queen. She owned over 2000 dresses and accessories like gloves, fans and scented handkerchiefs. Many of them were presents, because everyone knew she loved saving money almost as much as she loved clothes.

MEN IN HEELS

Louis XIV of France (1638–1715) was one of the most fashion-mad kings in history. He lived at his palace at Versailles with 5000 aristocrats (people from rich,

powerful families). Cosy. Louis loved gold
and silver coats, and he always wore silk
stockings and high-heeled shoes.
Maybe he liked to show off
his perfect legs. Or maybe,
self-conscious about being
short, he liked heels
that gave him a more
king-sized height. Because
Louis was the best-dressed man in
Europe, short and tall men copied his
high heels. A high, curved heel
is still called a 'Louis heel'.

THE LAST STAR

Probably the last royal fashion star was Princess Diana
(1961–1997). She was a shy kindergarten assistant
when she became engaged to Prince Charles, but she
soon became one of the world's most famous and
photographed celebrities. The public couldn't get
enough of her clothes, jewels and hairstyles, but the

glamorous princess had a serious side. She used the media focus to draw attention to many unfashionable causes, from landmine victims to leprosy. In June 1997, after her divorce from Prince Charles, she sent 79 of her gowns to be auctioned.

'Sequins save lives,' she said, donating the money – $3.25 million – to charity.

A couple of months later she was killed in a car crash.

2

foLLoWiNg the LeAder

SPREADING FASHION AROUND

Royal and rich people were the first fashion leaders,
but by the eighteenth century, actors and actresses,
singers, dancers and even writers and poets were
making fashion news. English poet Lord Byron
(1788–1824) was treated like a rock star. Mobs of
people gathered everywhere he went, and young men
copied his messy hair, open collar and loose necktie.

Lily Langtry (1853–1929) was a beautiful English
actress. Photographs and portraits of her were made

into postcards, making her the first 'pin-up' girl. Everything she wore made news, so designers loaded her with clothes. It meant free dresses for her, free advertising for them.

The American film industry based in Hollywood took off in the early 1920s, and soon movie stars were the new fashion leaders. When actor Clark Gable took his shirt off in a 1934 movie to show his bare chest underneath, men copied him and sales of singlets dropped. Mothers inflicted curlers on their daughters so they would look like curly-top child star Shirley Temple. A New York store sold 500 000 frilly dresses copied from one worn by actress Joan Crawford in a film. And one star had a hairstyle to die for.

fashion victim #1
LAKE'S LOCKS

The 1940s American movie star Veronica Lake (1919–1973) was famous for her long blonde hair with its floppy 'peek-a-boo' fringe. So many girls working in wartime factories copied her that there was an outbreak of accidents. They were getting their hair caught in the machines. So the US Government made an official request to her studio – could she please change her style? In her next movie she wore her hair pulled back in a bun, and that was the end of Lake's lethal locks.

CELEBRITY SELLS

Fashion and celebrity still go together. Video music clips, TV shows, movies and magazines make it easy to check out the stars and what they're wearing.

Thanks to hi-tech clothes manufacturers in Hong Kong and China, celebrity clothes can be copied and in the shops in just a couple of weeks. Lots of fashions start this way.

Performers also turn themselves into brands to sell more than just CDs and movies. American singer and actress Jennifer Lopez has J. Lo clothes and her own perfume, and Australian pop star Kylie Minogue has 'Love Kylie' undies. Fame is good for business!

THE KING OF FASHION

Sometimes designers are stars, too. An Englishman based in Paris, Charles Worth (1825–1895), was known as 'the king of fashion'. Before Worth, designers would visit ladies at their homes. Worth expected his clients to come to him. And they did – even though he was bossy and rude – because he designed such elegant clothes.

Worth *did* visit royalty. He designed clothes for nine European queens, and his most famous client was the Empress Eugénie (1826–1920), the beautiful wife of Napoleon III of France.

She loved Worth's crinoline gowns. Their huge skirts used enormous amounts of material. The fabric-makers of France loved them, too!

Worth had his own showroom, called a salon, and models to show off his creations. Customers came to choose clothes, have them fitted and then sewn specially for them. This kind of fashion is called *haute couture,* which means 'high-class sewing' in French.

Worth was the first super-star designer and he set the pattern for French fashion designers for the next century. Women all over the world looked to Paris for clothes that were elegant, new – and sometimes shocking.

HOBBLE TROUBLE

Designer Paul Poiret (1879–1944) outraged and excited the fashion world when he introduced bright colours, luxurious fabrics and exotic styles such as harem pants, kimonos and dresses without corsets. He boasted that he freed women from clothes that restricted movement. But then he went and invented the hobble skirt!

A hobble is a strap tied between a horse's legs so it can take only small steps and can't run away. Poiret made skirts so tight at the ankles that some women even wore a thing called a 'hobble garter' so they wouldn't step too far and split their skirts. It was like wearing handcuffs for the legs.

GO, COCO!

The 1920s saw the rise of female fashion designers. One of the most famous was Coco Chanel (1883–1971). No hobble skirts or corsets for Coco – she wanted women to feel relaxed and comfortable, so she designed easy-to-wear clothes, often based on sportswear. Glamorous Coco was her own best model. Suntans, knitted material, short hair, and simple skirts and jackets worn with fake jewellery all became popular because of her.

MY MUM'S COAT

Usually fashions come and go gradually. But Paris designer Christian Dior (1905–1957) was responsible for a fashion earthquake that totally changed the way women dressed – even thousands of kilometres away, in Melbourne, Australia!

In the winter of 1948, my mum had a beautiful new woollen coat, short and straight, with padded shoulders. Then 'The New Look' hit.

Dior figured that women were sick of the uniform-like fashions left over from World War II. So he gave them tiny waists, sloping shoulders and long, full skirts using metres and metres of material. They loved it! Journalists called it 'The New Look'. In Britain, where material and clothing were still scarce after World War II, the Government asked women not to wear the new fashion. No way! It was a fashion revolution. My mum wore her coat only a few times. With everyone else wearing Dior's New Look, Mum's old look just looked silly.

FASHION FOR EVERYBODY

Designers like Chanel and Dior had an influence that spread far beyond the exclusive world of haute couture. Though only a few wealthy customers actually bought their clothes, millions wore styles inspired by them. Magazines and newspapers reported the new styles at the twice-yearly fashion shows. Buyers from big stores attended. Soon cheaper copies were on sale in the shops. Fashion still filters down like this today.

Probably only about 1500 people world-wide buy haute couture clothes, because prices start at $37 240 for a simple dress and an evening gown could cost $745 000.

Today, advances in technology – like synthetic and stretch materials, computerised machines for cutting out and sewing – mean clothes can be mass-produced cheaply and quickly. Youth fashion – like punk, goth and surf – influences haute couture! Fashion isn't just for the rich, it's for everybody.

3

SHAPE-SHIFTING

SQUEEZING, PADDING AND ADDING ON

Imagine this: you put on a pair of bike shorts a size too small.

Tight?

Not tight enough. Add a pair of cut-off jeans, two sizes too small.

Still not tight enough. Breathe in, put on a wide belt and pull it – you guessed – *tight*. Now do up the buckle. Last, stick a couple of steel rulers down the sides.

That might give you some idea of what it was like to wear a corset.

THE BIG SQUEEZE

Women started wearing corsets in the 1500s. Corsets were made of stiffened cloth or leather with strips of whalebone or even metal sewn into the seams. They were rigid and uncomfortable, but it was the laces that caused the real squeeze. With laces, you could reduce your waist size by one-third. Some corsets were like wide belts. Others were more like stiff, lace-up singlets. The most extreme, which created the weird S-look of the late nineteenth century, extended over the bottom and half-way down the thighs. It was hard to sit down without snapping the whalebones. Ouch!

Corsets were tough to wear. They stopped women from exercising and relaxing; they made it hard to digest food, breathe and even sit down.

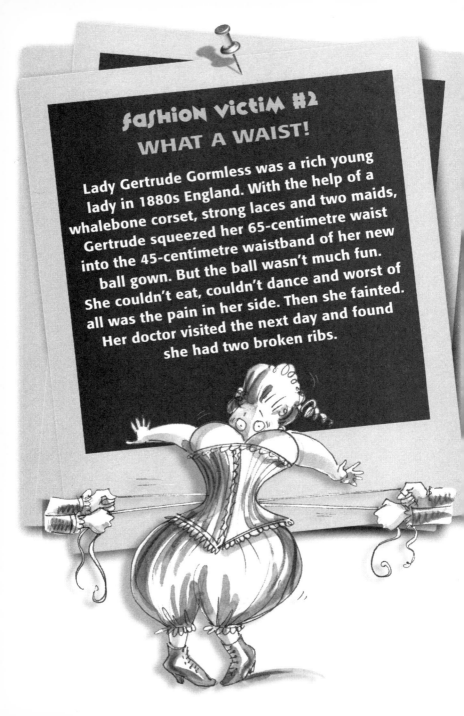

faShion Victim #2
WHAT A WAIST!

Lady Gertrude Gormless was a rich young lady in 1880s England. With the help of a whalebone corset, strong laces and two maids, Gertrude squeezed her 65-centimetre waist into the 45-centimetre waistband of her new ball gown. But the ball wasn't much fun. She couldn't eat, couldn't dance and worst of all was the pain in her side. Then she fainted. Her doctor visited the next day and found she had two broken ribs.

TIGHT-LACED LADIES — AND MEN

Could corsets really kill? Doctors lectured on the dangers of tight lacing, and there are stories of young women dying from punctured lungs or livers, but they may just be anti-corset propaganda. Many women actually believed that their bodies needed support from corsets. Even little girls wore them.

So did men. Whenever male fashions were tight-fitting, men with big tummies resorted to the corset. One famous corset-wearer was the Prince of Wales, George IV (1762–1830). He loved food and fashion, but unfortunately even a massive lace-up corset couldn't hide his bursting breeches. Cruel people called him the Prince of Whales. By the early twentieth century, men didn't care how big they were. In fact, a big tummy was a sign of wealth and power.

When King Edward VII (1841–1910) became too fat to do up his bottom waistcoat button, he left it undone. It became the fashion, and it still is today.

However, women wore corsets right into the twentieth century. When World War I broke out in 1914, women were needed as nurses, drivers and workers of all kinds, so loose, practical styles were worn. Women didn't climb back into corsets again until Christian Dior introduced the tight-waisted 'New Look' after World War II. Made of elastic material, and re-named 'girdles', they were a lot kinder than the whalebone and laces of the past. Today, women can buy undies with stretchy lycra panels to keep their tummies under control.

PEASECODS AND BOMBAST

Men and women didn't just want to look thinner. If only the Prince of Whales had lived in sixteenth-century Spain. There, gentlemen wore an artificial pot belly, called a peasecod or goose-belly, and padded their pants. The stuffing, made of wool, cotton fluff or animal hair,

was called bombast. Some men
even used bran or sawdust.
Bad idea. If you sat on a
nail and ripped your
pants, all your stuffing
would trickle out
onto the floor.
Men have
also padded out their chests, shoulders and even calves
to make them look bigger.

BUSTLES AND BUM-BARRELS

Women have mainly padded their hips and breasts.
In the sixteenth and seventeenth centuries women
wore a bum-barrel, a sausage-shaped cushion, tied
round their waists to make their skirts stick out.
In the late nineteenth century, women used a bustle
– a rounded horsehair pad tied to the waist – to create
a great big behind. A dress complete with bustle,
frills, bows and swags of material could weigh over
10 kilograms!

Women also wore wool or cotton pads called 'bust improvers' to give them big bosoms. Today, women can wear bras with pads or even gel inserts.

FASHION FRAMEWORKS

If you really want to stick out, padding just won't do. You need scaffolding. So women used whalebone, metal and wicker to create a totally new shape below the waist. An alien visitor would have wondered what women were hiding underneath their huge skirts.

The Spanish farthingale, worn right through the sixteenth century, was adopted in much of Europe. It was like a petticoat of stiff cloth set with hoops of wicker or whalebone. It held the skirt out in a stiff cone. In England, ladies liked a flat-topped drum shape.

From 1690 to 1780, women wore panniers. *Pannier* is the French word for basket, and that's what panniers under a dress were like – wicker or cane shapes that tied around the waist and stuck out at the side. The front and back were flat. This fashion even had

an effect on architecture. Double doors opened wide, and balustrades on staircases were curved so women could get close enough to hold the rail.

LADY IN A CAGE

In the early 1850s, women wore five or six heavy layers of stiff petticoats to hold their skirts out. But in 1856 an invention called the cage crinoline made life a little easier. The crinoline was a framework of flexible steel hoops, joined by vertical bands of tape. It was cheap, light and easy to wear, and both rich and poor women loved it. Soon skirts ballooned to crazy sizes – up to five metres around. Two women couldn't go through a door together. Coaches and railway carriages were very squeezy. In spite of this, the crinoline was in fashion for at least ten years.

Remember the bustle? Bustles went in and out of style a couple of times. In the 1880s, they were so big, it looked as though women were hiding the back half of a horse under their dresses. Horsehair pads would have been too heavy, so light metal frames were used. There was even a hi-tech, spring-loaded version. If a lady wanted to sit she raised it, and it automatically sprang back down when she stood up.

fashion victim #5
A WALK ON THE WIDE SIDE

Mademoiselle Adèle Derrière was a lady of the Court of Louis XV of France in 1755, and panniers nearly ruined her love life. Adèle's panniers were 5 metres across. She could hardly sit down, even in specially designed chairs with extra width and no arms, and she had to enter rooms sideways like a crab. Worst of all, she couldn't reach the hand of her fiancé, Count Louis Fromage. Luckily this extreme style was only worn at court, so they got to hold hands at home.

SHAPING UP

Though crinolines and peasecods are no longer daily wear, men and women still want to change their shapes. Today's fashions – like low-slung jeans, cropped tops and tight shirts – reveal the body. You can't fake muscles or a tiny waist with corsets and padding. So some people turn to extreme diet and exercise plans, steroids (artificial growth hormones) and even surgery to get the shape they want. Anorexia – an illness where people starve themselves to become thin – is increasing. Maybe that's because fashion models are so thin. One US study shows that models weigh 25 per cent less than the average women.

Perhaps corsets weren't so bad, after all!

4

MeN iN tightſ

FROM CODPIECE
TO THREE-PIECE

Check out these words: fop, popinjay, coxcomb, dandy, beau, exquisite, macaroni. Before you reach for the dictionary, I'll tell you – they're all ways of saying fashion addict. (Male fashion addict, that is.)

For most of European history, men have been peacocks. Men as well as women enjoyed lace, furs, jewels, bright colours, loud patterns, high heels, make-up and outrageous hats. But did you know that for most of history, only men wore tights? Tights for women first appeared in the 1960s.

TIGHT AND TIGHTER

European men didn't start
wearing long trousers till the
early 1800s. Before that, they wore
short breeches. And before that, back
in the 1300s, men wore hose. Today
we call them tights. The first tights
were made as two separate stockings,
tailored from cloth and laced onto
the bottom of the wearer's tunic.
The gap between the legs was filled with a pouch
of material called a codpiece.

NO FLIES ON THESE GUYS

Today, men have flies. (We're talking trousers,
not insects.) Back then, they had the codpiece.
(Cod means bag, not fish.) Originally, it was just a
lightly padded flap of material used to fill the gap
between the two separate legs of men's tights. Over
time, codpieces became an eye-catching accessory.

In the sixteenth century, codpieces were heavily padded so that they stuck out from the rest of the clothes, and were decorated with ribbons, puffs, slashes and even jewelled pins. They also doubled as purses.

The fashion died out around the end of the sixteenth century, and not surprisingly, it's never been revived.

STUFFED SHOES

In the late 1300s, sometimes soles were added to the feet of the tights and a fashion for lengthening the toes began. Especially in Poland. When King Richard II of England married Anne of Bohemia (whose kingdom included Poland) in 1382, the elegant courtiers who came with her amazed the English with their long, pointy shoes. People called them 'poulaines' (a mixed-up way of saying Polish). Poulaines became so long that the points had to be stiffened with whalebone or stuffed so the wearers could actually walk.

faſhion victim #4
SIR THOMAS AND HIS TOES

It was 1382, and stylish Sir Thomas Thingummy
was determined to have the longest toes at the
English court. His were 50 centimetres long
and tapering to a fine point. They looked great,
but even stuffed, they were totally unwalkable.
But he didn't give up. He attached gold chains
from the tips of his shoes to bands tied
to a jewelled garter just below the knee.
Unfortunately the priest objected. Sir Thomas
could not kneel to say his prayers.
Eventually laws were passed limiting
the length of pointy toes.

OBJECTION

In the fifteenth and sixteenth centuries, tights got tighter because knitted fabric became available. Especially in Italy, fashionable men liked to show off their legs with striped tights, or with legs of different colours, or even with half plain, half patterned legs. Breeches (pants ending at the knees) and stockings took over from full-leg tights by the seventeenth century. Garters, worn with tights or stockings, were a top male fashion accessory. They could be gold and jewelled, made of fringed silk or velvet, or even decorated with bunches of ribbons.

REAL MEN WEAR LACE

Queen Elizabeth I of England loved to have handsome and fashionable men around her court. Luckily, her courtiers also loved to dress up. They chose richly embroidered silks, satins and velvets for their padded breeches, doublets and capes; fine linen and lace for their shirts and ruffs; the sleekest tights for their legs. They grew beards, which they plaited and even dyed red in honour of their red-headed queen. They wore earrings, necklaces and rings, waved scented handkerchiefs, and carried swords in jewelled scabbards.

They used them, too. Sir Walter Raleigh, the adventurer who founded Virginia in America, and Sir Francis Drake, the Admiral who defeated the Spanish fleet, were just two of Elizabeth's courtiers. Though they liked fine clothes, they didn't live for fashion.

It was a different story for many gentlemen two hundred years later.

FASHION CLUBS

Two famous fashion clubs for men were the Macaronis and the Incroyables. The Macaroni Club was founded in London in 1764. Its mission? To promote over-the-top fashion, like tall powdered wigs, miniature three-cornered hats, shirts with huge lacy ruffles and tight coats, waistcoats and breeches.

Club members wore make-up and fake beauty spots, drenched themselves in perfume, and tottered about on high heels. The Macaronis were laughed at, abused and even beaten up.

The French Revolution, which began in 1789, swept away the rich and outrageous fashions of the French court. They were replaced by plain middle-class clothes for men and simple gowns for women.

But this was France! These plain clothes couldn't last. In the late 1790s, a group of young dandies called the Incroyables appeared in Paris. (*Incroyable* is French for incredible.)

faShion victim #3
INCREDIBLE PIERRE

Decisions, decisions! Pierre Lapin agonised over his outfit. Eventually he chose a tight, brown high-waisted jacket and a yellow waistcoat with huge lapels. Then he put on red-and-green striped breeches tied at the bottom with yellow ribbons. A huge hat was perched lopsided on his raggedly cut hair. He finished with low shoes, white stockings, flashy gold earrings and an enormous necktie wrapped six times around his neck, covering his chin and almost immobilising his head. He ignored the rude comments and laughter as he walked the streets of Paris. He knew he looked absolutely *incroyable*.

'BEAU' BRUMMELL

In the late eighteenth and early nineteenth century English men's fashion led Europe, and English men's fashion was led by George 'Beau' Brummell (1778–1840). Many men, including his fat friend George, Prince of Wales, tried to imitate his simple but elegant style, but few succeeded. Brummell carried stylish dressing to extremes. He took five hours to get dressed. He had three hairdressers – one for the sideburns, one for the front and one for the back – and polished his boots with champagne. A typical outfit was a blue coat, fawn waistcoat, pale pantaloons and tall highly polished boots. Under the influence of Beau Brummell, flashy styles and colours went out of style for men. And stayed that way.

SUITABLE CLOTHES

For the next 150 years, men's fashion was ruled by the three-piece suit. Trousers, jacket and waistcoat, that is. Men didn't have to ask themselves, 'What will I wear?' The suit was nearly always suitable. Wealthy gentlemen had theirs sewn and fitted by tailors: ordinary men bought them ready-made. Colours were usually dull, such as black, grey or dark blue.

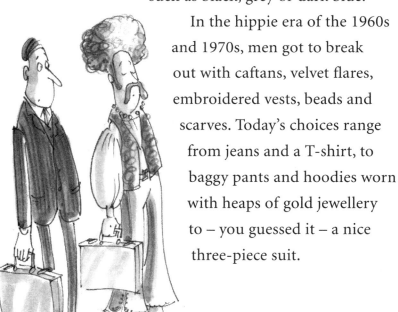

In the hippie era of the 1960s and 1970s, men got to break out with caftans, velvet flares, embroidered vests, beads and scarves. Today's choices range from jeans and a T-shirt, to baggy pants and hoodies worn with heaps of gold jewellery to – you guessed it – a nice three-piece suit.

5

butterflies
and bigwigs

THE LONG AND SHORT
OF HATS AND HAIR

High hats and even higher hair have often been worn by the rich and powerful, and when you think about it, a big head does make you stand out in the crowd.

People also just thought big heads looked good. What do you think?

HOOD HISTORY

Men's hat history starts with the hood. The hood is just a tube with an opening for the face, and a point at the back. Warm, practical and simple – until fashion got hold of it. During the 1300s, the point lengthened into a long tail that was wrapped or tied around the head. Then it was stuffed. A sausage up to two metres in length – called a liripipe – dangled down, was held in the hand or draped around the body.

Next, fashionable men started wearing the face opening on the top of the head and rolling the neck part up to make a kind of brim. Then they took the whole thing off the head altogether and wore it as a kind of weird scarf. By the 1400s, the hood was a total mutant. The merry men would have run a mile if Robin Hood had tried this one on. Next time you wear a hoodie or pull on a beanie, remember it all started 700 years ago.

BULBS AND FLOWERPOTS

Hat-wearing took off in the 1400s, and wealthy men could choose from an amazing variety of shapes. Cones, bulbs, upturned flowerpots, loaves, floppy cushions and turban styles were worn, and decorations included feathers, jewels and ribbons. Felt made from wool or beaver fur and velvet were the favourite materials. Large floppy felt hats with feathers – think of pirates and musketeers – were worn in the seventeenth century. Eighteenth-century men wore three-cornered hats called tricorns. In the nineteenth century, rich and powerful men all over Europe and America wore top hats. Middle-class men wore small hats. Workers often wore flat caps, and they had to take them off in the presence of those tall-hatted gentlemen. As with

most of men's clothing, by the twentieth century hats
had become very plain. Hardly anyone wears a 'topper'
today, except hotel doormen and guests at fancy
weddings.

HORNS AND BUTTERFLIES

Women's hat history is just as varied. Until the early
1960s no well-dressed woman would leave the house
without a hat – or a bonnet, turban, mobcap, boater,
cloche, pill-box or toque. They are just some of the
many different shapes and styles. In the 1930s fashion
designer Elsa Schiaparelli even created hats shaped
like a shoe and a lamb chop. Probably the biggest
hats ever were worn in the late nineteenth and early
twentieth centuries. Their wide brims were loaded

down with lace, ribbons, fur, fake fruit and flowers, jewels, veils, feathers, birds' wings or even whole birds. Must have weighed a ton!

But the prize for the most amazing headgear goes to women in the fourteenth and fifteenth century.

Light frameworks formed gigantic horns, and glue and wire held out the stiffened veils of vast butterfly or winged head-dresses. Huge stuffed rolls were worn like a lifebelt around the head, or else bent into heart, saddle or U-shapes. Tall cones or steeples called hennins grew to enormous heights – up to a metre. Transparent or coloured veils were often worn, and hair was tucked away. Women shaved their hairlines and plucked their eyebrows and the backs of their necks. Their heads must have looked like huge eggs.

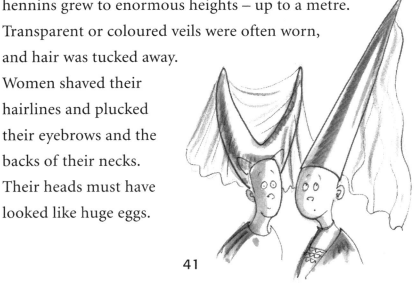

FONTANGES AND FIRE-TRAPS

Another high head-dress was the fontange, named after one of Louis XIV's girlfriends, Mademoiselle de Fontanges. Her hair got messy when they were out hunting one day, so she tied it back up with her garter. Louis thought she looked so lovely that he asked her to keep her hair that way. All the court ladies copied her, although the windy-day hair was turned into a head-dress up to 20 centimetres high, made of layers of pleated ruffles held up with wire. The fontange was popular in Europe from the 1680s to about 1710.

In the 1770s, women wore hair so high that sometimes it caught fire in the chandeliers. And no one had bigger hair than the English Duchess of Devonshire.

ITCHY AND SCRATCHY

These huge hairdos or wigs were powdered with flour or white starch. It made great food for lice and other insects, so a head-scratcher on a very long handle was needed. There are even stories of 'heads' being 'opened'

43

to reveal families of mice inside. Hot, heavy and itchy though they were, the hairdos were left for weeks, because they were so expensive and time-consuming to achieve.

Men wore powder on their own long hair or on small wigs, but a century earlier, men had also had huge hair – not only tall, but wide and long.

KING-SIZE HAIR

Under King Louis XIV, France was the most powerful nation in Europe. Louis was nicknamed the Sun King – and he must have looked dazzling dressed up in his gold and silver coats, jewels, gold shoe-buckles and lace. He had everything he wanted. Except one thing: hair. He was going bald. So he started wearing a wig.

Louis was quite short, so his wigs were very high to make him look taller. Soon every fashionable man in Europe had followed his lead. Wigs became a symbol of male dignity and power.

BIGWIGS

Periwigs (later shortened to wig) were very large and heavy, a mass of curls and ringlets which rose from either side of a centre parting and flowed down over the shoulders and back nearly to the waist. Rich men wore wigs instead of their natural hair from 1660 till around 1800, and high-quality human hair wigs were an expensive status symbol. In 1665, when bubonic plague was sweeping through London, there were rumours that hair was being cut from the corpses of plague victims to make wigs. Scary! In eighteenth-century Europe, hair was so valuable that it could be risky for children to go out alone in case their hair was cut off and stolen.

Today judges still wear wigs as symbols of authority in some countries, and 'bigwig' is a cheeky name for an important person.

DREAD HEADS

Probably the biggest hair you'll see today is a Rasta hairdo. Rasta is short for Rastafarian – a follower of an Afro-Caribbean religion. The look is achieved by letting the hair mat and knot into long locks called dreadlocks or 'dreads'. Dreads are supposed to symbolise the mane of a lion. Westerners first saw dreads on the heads of reggae musicians and singers like Bob Marley in the 1970s, and started matting their hair for fashion, not religion. There have been many unconfirmed reports of fashion victims with redback spiders in their dreads.

6

FASHION crimes

LAWS TO CONTROL CLOTHES

You're walking down the street on your way to a party. You're looking good in your scarlet velvet leggings, gold top, purple silk cloak and boots trimmed with leopard fur.

Suddenly a loud voice booms, 'Stop right there. You're busted!'

'F-f-for what?' you stammer.

'Fashion crimes,' comes the stern reply.

'What?'

'It's the purple, the scarlet, the silk, the fur, the gold. You know the law. I'm taking you in!'

SUMPTUARY LAWS

That little scene probably never happened – but it could have if you lived in England in the 1500s. Elizabeth I made a whole set of laws about what you could and could not wear. They were called sumptuary laws.

For example, no one except the royal family was allowed to wear purple silk, cloth of gold or sable (a kind of fur). Luxury materials such as silk, satin, velvet and gold and silver tissue, imported and rare furs, trimmings such as embroidery and jewels – even colours like purple and red – were strictly rationed according to who you were and how much money you had.

MIRROR, MIRROR

Mirror, mirror on the wall,
I should be best dressed of all.

If they weren't saying it,
they were thinking it.
Kings and queens all over
Europe made sumptuary laws.
Philippe IV of France (1268–1314) forbade dukes,
counts, barons and their wives to own more than four
garments, and unmarried women could only have one
unless they were heiresses to a castle. This crackdown
obviously didn't work. When Philippe's wife Jeanne
entered the city of Bruges in 1301, all the well-dressed
locals came out into the streets to greet her. 'I thought
I was the Queen,' she said, 'but I see there are hundreds.'

WHO'S WHO

Historians can't find much evidence that sumptuary
laws were strictly enforced – so why were they made?
Mainly to show who was who. With their castles and

mansions, city properties and huge estates with farms and forests, the noble families had lots of money and power. They were the upper or ruling class.

But from the late thirteenth century the rapidly growing middle class of merchants and traders were also getting richer, and so were able to afford the materials and styles of the nobility. Sumptuary laws show that the upper classes were worried about these changes in society. If you can't tell a rich merchant from a rich duke, what is the world coming to?

While some laws were about keeping people in their places, others were made to help their countries by forcing people to buy home-made rather than imported materials. One example 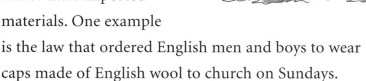 is the law that ordered English men and boys to wear caps made of English wool to church on Sundays. These laws weren't always a success.

DECORATION CRACKDOWN

Cardinal Jules Mazarin (1602–61) was a statesman under King Louis XIII of France. In 1656, worried by the amount of waste and extravagance in France, he passed laws forbidding the use of gold and silver as decoration. Result? Everyone hated him! Not just the rich elegant people who *wanted* to waste their money on gold and silver buttons, buckles, braid and embroidery, but the poor struggling workers who made them. The laws were going to ruin their industries. The crackdown turned into a backdown, and the laws were quickly repealed.

ARE YOUR LEGS LEGAL?

Another set of laws were made to protect people from seeing women's legs. In 1850s France, for example, a woman who wanted to wear trousers had to get government permission. In Bavaria during World War I,

51

women were forbidden to wear trousers except while skiing. And in the USA in the 1920s, several states tried to legislate dress lengths. Utah women wearing skirts more than 7.5 centimetres above the ankle could be fined – or even put in jail.

These laws were designed to protect 'public decency' – to stop people from being shocked. Things have loosened up since then, but in most countries it's still against the law to walk around naked – except on special beaches.

IN THE SWIM

What to wear on the beach has caused a lot of fuss over the years. Until the 1900s, men and women swam separately. Men usually swam naked. Women wore heavy 'bathing dresses' that covered up as much of the body as possible. Sometimes they were wheeled out into the waves in carts called 'bathing machines' so no one could even see them entering the water.

As swimming became more popular for both men and women, men started to swim in all-in-one suits, singlets and shorts or brief V-shaped trunks.

BATTLE OF THE BEACH

Australia . . . so many beaches! And in the early 1900s, so many rules! On many beaches, 'mixed bathing' (men and women swimming together) was banned, swimming was only allowed during certain times, sunbaking was forbidden and swimmers had to cover up. Totally. Those V-trunks had to go!

In 1907, the mayors of three Sydney beach suburbs decided to take a stand. They decreed that all swimmers had to wear a top with sleeves to the elbow, pants reaching to the knees and a skirt covering the hips. There was an uproar from young men. No way were they going to swim in skirts!

Surfers at Bondi and Manly staged demonstrations, marching along wearing all kinds of silly petticoats, skirts and dresses. They made their point, and soon a costume consisting of a dark knitted singlet and shorts became standard wear for everyone on Australian beaches. Briefer and more sensible bathing wear evolved over the twentieth century – but still not everybody was happy.

BEACH ILLEGAL 1

Annette Kellermann (1887–1975) was a famous Australian swimmer. When she went for a dip in Boston in 1907, she wore a one-piece jersey bathing suit.

It was sleeveless, but had a high neck and came to the knees. She was arrested for indecent exposure.

BEACH ILLEGAL II

In 1961 Miss Joan Barry was ordered from Bondi beach and later fined £3 for offensive behaviour. Her crime? Wearing a small bikini. Council regulations stated that there must be at least 3 inches (7.5 centimetres) of material at the sides of a bikini bottom.

Beach inspectors roved the sands with tape measures on the lookout for illegal bikinis.

7

kids' clothes

FROM SWADDLING BANDS TO SILLY SUITS

You're lucky. If you'd been born 500 years ago, you would have been a fashion victim for sure. Even if you'd been born 150 years ago, things could have been tough. Have a look.

ALL WRAPPED UP

Imagine you're a baby. You want to kick your legs and play with your toes. But they've wrapped you up tightly in long thick bandages, fastened with pins.

Your nappy is very full. It takes such a long time to wrap and unwrap you, they don't change you very often. You're itchy but you can't even wriggle. It's hard to cry because it's hard to breathe. And when they pick you up, it doesn't feel like a cuddle.

THE STORY OF SWADDLING

The baby's bandages were called swaddling bands; they date back to ancient Rome and were used in most of Europe until well into the 1700s. Babies were wrapped up like mini-mummies, sometimes strapped onto boards or straw mattresses.

Why did they do it? Well, people thought that babies might scratch their eyes out. Or that their arms and legs could fall off, or grow crooked.

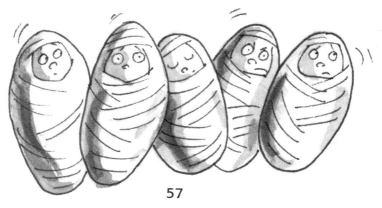

They might thrash about so hard their heads would come off. They might even get into a violent rage and hurt someone! It's true – people really did think these things. Babies were swaddled for at least the first two months, and sometimes for as much as a year.

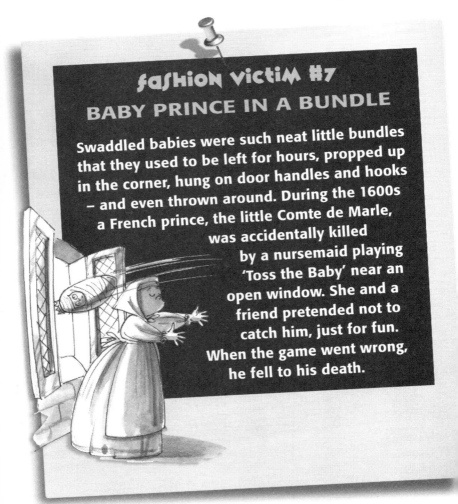

fashion victim #7
BABY PRINCE IN A BUNDLE

Swaddled babies were such neat little bundles that they used to be left for hours, propped up in the corner, hung on door handles and hooks – and even thrown around. During the 1600s a French prince, the little Comte de Marle, was accidentally killed by a nursemaid playing 'Toss the Baby' near an open window. She and a friend pretended not to catch him, just for fun. When the game went wrong, he fell to his death.

NICE DRESS, FRED

All small children wore dresses or gowns until the early 1900s. When you look at old photographs or portraits, that cute little girl in the frilly dress may well actually be a boy. Dresses and gowns for wearing at home were usually fairly plain and sensible, but little children wore elaborate bonnets, petticoats, frills, lace, sashes and ribbons on special occasions.

Leading strings – ribbons attached to the back of the armholes – were used to control toddlers' movements.

BRINGING UP BABIES

Most adults didn't understand that babies and children need to play and explore. Many rich parents didn't even look after their own children. They employed women called wet-nurses to breast-feed their babies, and nurses to look after them until they were at least three. The baby was often sent out to the nurse's home, and sometimes children did not see their own parents before they were five or six. Things didn't get much better for children until fashions in child-rearing started to change in the late 1700s.

faʃHioN VictiM #6
THE IRON CORSET

Worst of all, some children were laced into corsets. People believed that they would help the child's body to grow straight. When in 1665 little Elizabeth Evelyn died, the doctor and surgeon who examined her found she had two broken ribs and squashed organs. The doctor told her father that her 'iron bodice' had stopped her lungs from growing.

Her corset had killed her. She was only two years old.

MINI-ME

Once children reached somewhere between six and eight, they were dressed as adults.

That meant farthingales, corsets, peasecod bellies, ruffs, doublets, panniers – if it was in fashion for the adults, then it was for the kids. Boys were 'breeched' at the age of six or seven. That meant being taken out of dresses and taken away from nurses and mother to join the men. Up to the seventeenth century, wealthy boys also got their first sword at that age.

Girls started helping their mothers with household work – which was a serious job in the days when just about everything was home-made.

Now they were dressed like adults, children were expected to behave like them too.

NO FUN ALLOWED

They were often harshly punished for things like running, jumping and shouting – just for being kids. 'Spare the rod and spoil the child' was an often-quoted proverb.

From the late 1700s to around 1825 boys wore a 'skeleton suit'. It was nothing to do with bones – it was a shirt with a frilled collar, ankle-length pants and a short jacket worn with flat shoes and white socks. Girls got to wear shorter dresses with pantalettes (long pants with lace or frills at the hem). Sometimes the dresses were versions of women's styles (complete with corset) but at least the length made it easier to walk and run.

fashion victim #9
CEDRIC AND HIS SILLY SUIT

'I won't.'

'You will, Freddy.'

'I won't!'

'Cedric looked beautiful in that suit, Freddy, and so will you.'

'I won't!'

He did. You have to feel sorry for him, dressed in that black velvet suit with its floppy lace collar, knee-length pants, wide sash and a big plumed hat. You don't have to feel sorry for Cedric. Cedric was just the hero of a book, a best-seller called *Little Lord Fauntleroy* by Frances Hodgson Burnett. It inspired many mothers to dress their boys like Cedric, and his look was popular – especially for parties – from 1886 well into the 1890s. Popular with mothers, that is.

MY LITTLE SWEETUMS

Sailor suits were especially popular in England and Germany, two countries with strong navies. They were worn by boys and girls from around 1840 right into the twentieth century.

CLOTHES FOR KIDS

Starting in the early twentieth century, children's clothes became more comfortable and easier to wear. No more fashion victims. When you think of some styles we've looked at, you can see how lucky kids are today. Stretchy, light materials and styles like jeans, track pants, shorts and T-shirts make it much easier to be a kid.

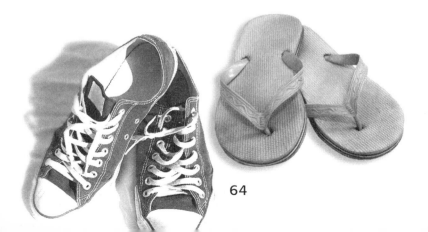

8

the real victims

SAD BUT TRUE TALES OF SUFFERING

Fashion can be murder. It's true! Murder, wars, kidnapping, cruelty . . . here are some of the real fashion victims.

CRUELTY AND FASHION

To many people, fashion cruelty means fur. Let's face it, you can't wear fur without killing the animal that was wearing it first. The demand for fur has been so great that some animals were hunted until they were rare or even extinct. Starting in the late twentieth century, groups like Greenpeace have turned people off fur by showing pictures of baby seals being clubbed and foxes caught in leg traps.

Even though fur is produced today with less cruelty and more care for the environment, the fur trade is tiny compared to what it has been. Did you know that the quest for fur has been responsible for wars and invasions? Blame it on the beaver.

GOLD-MINE OF FUR

Felt is made by wetting, heating, rolling and pressing fur, hair or wool. Unluckily for beavers, their fur made perfect felt. From around 1550, hatters made beaver felt into hard-wearing but very fashionable hats – so fashionable that by the early 1600s, there were hardly any beavers left in Europe.

But there were millions in North America.

Starting in the 1600s, the quest for beavers drove the invasion, exploration and settlement of vast areas of land. Not just beavers, but foxes, lynx, martens, wolves, seals, and many other fur-bearing animals were found there in huge numbers. North America was a gold-mine of fur – and worth fighting for. Traditional enemies France and England competed for control for over 150 years. (The English won the country now called Canada).

The native people – First Nations and Inuit tribes – were vital to the fur trade. The explorers and traders relied on them as guides and to supply furs. But the fur trade created competition and wars between tribes and disrupted their traditional lifestyle. The traders also spread European diseases like smallpox, which wiped out over half the native population.

MOUNTAINS OF BIRDS

To decorate the enormous hats of the late nineteenth and early twentieth centuries, mountains of rare birds from all over the world were delivered to dealers

in Paris and
London. In 1890
a London dealer
received 32 000 hummingbirds,
80 000 water birds and 800 000 mixed
pairs of wings in just one delivery.

Ostrich feathers were also popular, but they could
be pulled out without killing the bird. Other birds
weren't so lucky.

ENDANGERED EGRETS

Take the egret. It lives in swampy areas
of North and South America, and its
plumes or 'aigrettes' are at their
peak during the breeding season.
Aigrettes were a favourite hat
decoration, and so birds were
shot while on their nests.

The chicks were left to starve, the eggs to rot. Whole colonies of egrets were wiped out. Why? – because aigrettes were worth twice their weight in gold.

FASHION VICTIM #10
HATS OF DEATH

It's 1902, and Miss Felicity Floss is trying on hats. She likes the one with the ostrich feathers, but then the one decorated with parrots' wings is so colourful.

'But look!' says Madame Poulet the milliner.

'How sweet!' says Miss Floss. A hat loaded with tiny little dead hummingbirds!

So off goes gentle Miss Floss, who wouldn't hurt a flea, wearing her brand-new hat of death.

More than a million egrets a year were killed by plumage hunters. Add the deaths of young and eggs, and you can see why this bird was in big trouble.

Though bird-lovers worked hard to create new laws and bird sanctuaries to protect the egret, what probably saved it was what nearly destroyed it – a change in fashion. By the 1920s, small plain hats were in and hats of death were history.

BLOOD-STAINED COTTON

Even cotton has a blood-stained history. In the eighteenth century England was famous for its textile industry. New machines were invented to spin and weave cotton quickly and cheaply. Large cotton plantations in England's southern American colonies supplied the raw materials, but the plantation owners needed more workers. There was already a thriving slave market in West Africa, supplied by local chiefs and slave traders. British merchants saw a great business opportunity.

TRIANGULAR TRADE

British ships sailed to Africa with goods like tools, material, weapons and jewellery. These were swapped for people. They sailed to America and the West Indies with the slaves chained in filthy conditions below decks. Many slaves did not survive. Those that did survive were sold. Then the traders sailed back to England with coffee, sugar, tobacco and cotton grown with slave labour. It was called the 'triangular trade', because it took three voyages. In this way, between 10 and 12 million people were separated from their families, forced to work and treated like animals.

Workers in the English cotton mills were also poorly treated. Children as young as seven worked long days and were often mangled or killed by the machines.

The cotton industry would never have made such huge profits without slave labour in America and cheap labour at home. Some of the cotton produced in this way was even traded back in West Africa for – you guessed it – more slaves.

SEWING MACHINES AND SWEATSHOPS

By the late nineteenth century, technological advances like machines for making textiles and the invention of the sewing machine meant fashion was now cheap and available to most people. They also led to a new kind of workplace. Formerly tailors and seamstresses had hand-sewn clothes in small workrooms, but from the 1850s the sewing machine opened the way for mass production. Now hundreds of workers, usually women, were crammed together making clothes. They were called 'sweatshops'.

That's just a few of the real fashion victims. Concerned men and women struggled to end the slave trade, send children to school instead of work, form unions, ensure that workers have safe workplaces and stop cruelty to animals in the name of fashion. The struggle still continues in some places today.

THE TRIANGLE
SHIRTWAIST WORKERS

The Triangle Shirtwaist Company employed
500 women and girls (the youngest was 13).
Their workrooms were on the top three floors
of a ten-storey building in New York. To stop
the women leaving their sewing machines, the
owners used to lock the doors. In 1911 when a
fire broke out, many of the women were trapped.
Though the fire brigade came quickly, nothing
went right. The ladders only reached to the
sixth floor. The fire escape collapsed. Women
fell while trying to slide down the lift cables,
while others, with
their dresses on fire,
jumped; the bodies got
in the way of the firemen.
The life nets broke.

It took just 15 minutes for
146 women to die.

WHAT'S NEW?

YOUTH AND TEENAGE FASHION

Recently I saw a teenage girl wearing a miniskirt and platform shoes. Seeing this girl brought back memories, horrible memories . . .

Platform shoes aren't new. Mega-platforms called chopines were worn by Italian ladies back in the sixteenth and seventeenth centuries. They were up to 60 centimetres high and those ladies needed a helper on either side so they could walk. When World War II caused a shortage of leather in the 1940s, women wore shoes with clumpy wood, cork and raffia soles. Platforms were big in the 1970s too – and that brings me back to my scary fashion flashback.

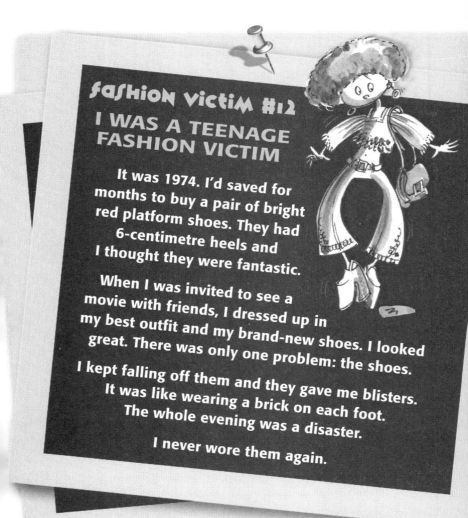

faSHioN ViCtiM #12
I WAS A TEENAGE FASHION VICTIM

It was 1974. I'd saved for months to buy a pair of bright red platform shoes. They had 6-centimetre heels and I thought they were fantastic.

When I was invited to see a movie with friends, I dressed up in my best outfit and my brand-new shoes. I looked great. There was only one problem: the shoes.

I kept falling off them and they gave me blisters. It was like wearing a brick on each foot. The whole evening was a disaster.

I never wore them again.

Miniskirts first came into fashion in the early 1960s, and they caused a huge fuss.

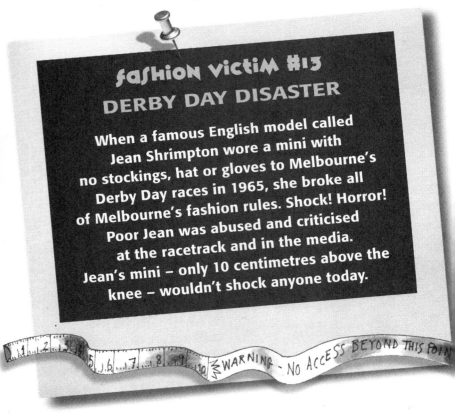

faShion Victim #13

DERBY DAY DISASTER

When a famous English model called Jean Shrimpton wore a mini with no stockings, hat or gloves to Melbourne's Derby Day races in 1965, she broke all of Melbourne's fashion rules. Shock! Horror! Poor Jean was abused and criticised at the racetrack and in the media. Jean's mini – only 10 centimetres above the knee – wouldn't shock anyone today.

WARNING – NO ACCESS BEYOND THIS POIN

Lots of fashions start out looking shocking on young people and teenagers, but end up OK on just about everybody, from little kids to grandparents. Older people have been shocked and offended by all sorts of styles, including miniskirts, jeans, work gear and athletics clothes worn as street wear, biker-style leather jackets and pants, Doc Marten boots, slogan T-shirts, shaved heads and heavy make-up. These days, you see a guy wearing a leather jacket and ripped jeans. So what? That girl's got a nose-ring. Big deal!

UGLY AND SCARY

Well, in the mid-1970s, clothes like that were worn by punk rockers or punks. In their music, behaviour and clothes, they set out to shock mainstream society. Lots of people thought punks looked ugly, scary and violent. Now, punk gear like black clothing, leather jackets, heavy boots, torn clothes, fishnet tights and piercing has turned tame. You can buy pre-ripped jeans, and only the more extreme styles – like bondage pants and spiked hair – stand out today.

Decorating the body with piercing, tattooing and scarring is centuries old and has been practised by tribal people all over the world. When the first punks appeared with pierced noses and safety pins in their ears, it was new and shocking. Now, over 25 years

later, piercing is no big deal. Studs, rings, and jewellery in the ears, nose, eyebrow and navel are common. Not a protest statement, a fashion statement.

fashioN VictiM #14
PIERCED TO DEATH

As usual, some people take fashion to extremes. Like a Welsh woman, 39-year-old Lesley Hovvels, who died of blood poisoning after having 118 piercings. Doctors commenting on her case reminded people that piercings are wounds, after all. They can bleed and scab up, and they'll become infected if you don't look after them.

RIP

SCARY STORIES

One woman nearly died when her tongue swelled and blocked her air supply after she reacted badly to her new tongue piercing. And another man damaged his mouth and gums so badly with his tongue jewellery that he needed skin grafts. But the story about the boy who was fried when his metal tongue stud acted as a lightning rod is just that – a story.

BACK IN BLACK

Looking at youth fashion can be like looking at different tribes. They each have their own look, language, music and lifestyle.

Take the goths. The essence of goth is black.
They wear black suits or dresses, dye their hair black,
and many goths look on the black side of life, too, with
an interest in darkness, death and the supernatural.
Other features are heavy make-up (white face, dark
eyes and lips) for males and females; silver jewellery
with crosses and skulls; clothes made from lace, leather
and velvet (black, of course!); heavy boots;
and even a return to Victorian styles
like corsets and bustles. Some goths
are serious people with beliefs
inspired by art, music
and poetry; others are
just having fun
dressing up.

CLOTHES, MUSIC AND A DJ

A big contrast to goth is hip-hop. Hip-hop music
started in inner-city America, at African-American
street parties and in clubs, when a DJ and a rapper

combined to make music.
Now teenagers all around
the world – especially boys
– listen to hip-hop or rap
music. Even more people
wear the styles.

Hip-hop style means
outsized baggy pants,
athletic gear, hooded jackets,
gold jewellery and running shoes.
It can also meant wearing dark
glasses day and night, and having your undies show
above the waistband of your jeans. Footwear is very
important. Kids have even been mugged and beaten up
for their expensive runners.

While goths often like to express themselves
by being different – making their clothes or finding
them in second-hand shops – in hip-hop culture it's
important to have the latest fashion and the coolest
designer brands. Rappers even talk about different
brands in their lyrics, giving designers and labels like
Tommy Hilfiger, Guess and Versace free advertising.

The place to see really wild teenage and youth fashion is at a dance party, club or rave. People who look pretty ordinary during the week blossom out into wild animals, fantasy creatures, gangsters, disco queens, babies (complete with glow-in-the-dark dummies!) and whatever else they want to be.

From teenage street fashion to haute couture, clothes express people's beliefs, attitudes and lifestyle. If you're interested in people, go fashion spotting. You'll see people who are in fashion, ahead of fashion (weird but good), old-fashioned and out of fashion (just weird).

You might even see a fashion victim.

One last story. It's about an American dancer called Isadora Duncan (1878–1927) who was famous for her flamboyant dresses and flowing scarves.

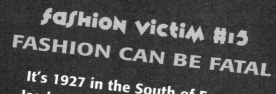

faShioN victiM #15
FASHION CAN BE FATAL

It's 1927 in the South of France. Isadora wraps her long silk scarf around her neck, gets into her car and off they go. But . . . something's wrong! The driver brakes, but it's too late. The trailing scarf had caught in the spoked rear wheel of the open-top car, strangling Isadora and yanking her right out of the vehicle. She's dead. Her clothes killed her.

SUSAN GREEN has been a teacher, radio producer, youth worker, cook, shop assistant, writer and part-time fashion victim. *It's True! Fashion Can Be Fatal* is her ninth book for children and young people. Susan lives in country Victoria with her husband, son, mum, a dog, a cat, six fish and four pythons. She's mainly to be found in jeans and work boots, but the crinoline comes out on special occasions.

GREGORY ROGERS still owns clothes that he wore back in the 1970s. Not that he wears them. He just thinks it's criminal to throw out something that isn't absolutely threadbare. In those days, his favourite pair of shoes were bubble-toe, platform-soled "Noddy" shoes in red, ochre and green. Looking back, he realises there is a thin line between making a statement and being a fashion tragedy.

THANKS

Thanks to the staff at Castlemaine Library for their help and patience.

Susan Green

The publishers would like to thank the following for photographs used in the text: istockphoto.com for those on pages i, vi, 47, 48, 64, 67, 78 and 79, and for the 'polaroids' and 'pins' used for Fashion Victims; La Trobe Picture Collection, State Library of Victoria, for those on pages 17, 62 and 68.

TIMELINE

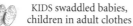

1200s

EUROPE fashion explosion – travellers, soldiers, traders bring new styles to court

KIDS swaddled babies, children in adult clothes

1300s

MEN tights, poulaines, codpieces and hoods

WOMEN head-dresses

1300s to 1600s

sumptuary laws

1400s

MEN hoods give way to hats, all shapes and sizes

'duck's beak' shoes

1500s

WOMEN first corsets, bum-barrels, farthingales, chopines

MEN stuffed and decorated codpieces, peasecods, padded breeches

underpants new to France

Queen Elizabeth I's courtiers wear jewellery, lace, scented handkerchiefs

beaver fur hats

1600s

quest for beaver fur begins fur trade in North America

MEN Louis XIV sets styles for Europe – especially high heels and wigs

MEN floppy hats with feathers

WOMEN fontange head-dresses and panniers

1700s

MEN tricorne hats

WOMEN hair towers

MEN fashion clubs

English textile industries expand – cotton imports, slave trade

1800s

MEN long trousers and suits; top-hats for the rich

WOMEN more petticoats, then cage crinoline, bustle and tight corsets

KIDS 'Little Lord Fauntleroy' suits

WOMEN bonnets, then huge hats with masses of trimmings and feathers

invention of sewing machine allows mass production of clothes

1900s

swimsuit scandals

WOMEN hobble skirts replaced by loose clothes

Hollywood stars start to set trends

WOMEN bikini inspectors and miniskirts

MEN more casual clothes (hippy gear, jeans)

Rasta hairstyles, punk, platform shoes

KIDS easy-to-wear, comfortable clothes

2000s

piercing

fashion tribes like goths and hip-hop

recycled styles like platform shoes, miniskirts

street fashion, rave and dance party fashion

WHERE TO FIND OUT MORE

Websites
- www.costumes.org/
- www.fashion-era.com/

Books
L. Rowland-Warne, *Costume*, Collins Eyewitness Guides series, CollinsAngus & Robertson Publishers, Sydney, 1992

Helen Whitty, *You Are What You Wear*, published for the Powerhouse Museum by Macmillan Education Australia, Melbourne, 2000
plus other books
in the same series

Accessories and Adornment

Dressing Up

Hats, Gloves and Footwear

Protective Clothing

Underwear

Robyn Healy, *Fashion and Textiles*, Council of Trustees of the National Gallery of Victoria, Melbourne, 2003, has good close-up photographs of costume detail

For current fashion, look at fashion, music and entertainment magazines.

INDEX